Water
under
Water

Charles Adés Fishman

Published by Casa de Snapdragon Publishing LLC
A Traditional, Independent Publishing Company
MMIX

Cover photo copyright/acknowledgement Cynthia Berridge. Author photo courtesy of Ellen Marcie Fishman.

Library of Congress Cataloging-in-Publication Data

Fishman, Charles Adés.
  Water under water / Charles Adés Fishman.
    p. cm.
  Poems.
  ISBN 978-0-9840530-2-5 (pbk.)
  I. Title.

PS3606.I83W37 2009
811'.6--dc22

Published by
Casa de Snapdragon LLC
12901 Bryce Avenue NE
Albuquerque, NM 87112
https://www.casadesnapdragon.com

Printed in the United States of America

For Lynn Strongin
my northwesternmost sister:
love & admiration

Acknowledgments

My thanks to the editors of the following periodicals, in which some of the poems in this book (often in earlier versions) first appeared: *Abiko Quarterly, American Literary Review, American Writing, Amicus Journal* (later *OnEarth*), *Beloit Poetry Journal, Big City Lit, Boulevard, Caesura, Calapooya Collage, Confluence, Confrontation, Connecticut Review, Cottonwood Review, Dalhousie Review, Gander Press Review, Georgia Review, Grain, Hart, Hawaii Pacific Review, Hawai'i Review, JBStillwater.com, Kota Press Poetry Journal, Laurel Review, Long Island Quarterly, Louisiana Literature, Magnolia, Mannequin Envy, Men As We Are, Muse Apprentice Guild, New Letters, New Works Review, Pacific International, Passager, Pearl, Petroglyph, poetrymagazine.com, Poetry Porch, Sunstorm, TheScreamOnline, Williwaw, Wordsmith,* and *Words-Myth.*

"Field" first appeared in *The Arvon Poetry Competition Anthology*, ed. Ted Hughes and Seamus Heaney (Kilnhurst Publishing Company, 1982); "At Browning's Pond," "Fathers Are Not Stones," "July 1946" and "Sun and Rain" in *Zoom* (Singular Speech Press, 1990); "By the Sea," "Sand Burial," "Speaking Island," and "In the Wave" in *As the Sun Goes down in Fire*, winner of the 1992 Anabiosis Press Chapbook Competition; "The Dream"(originally "The Message") in *To Woo and to Wed: Poets on Love & Marriage*, ed. Michael Blumenthal (Poseidon Press, 1992); "Flood Tide" in *Parnassus of World Poets*, ed. Ramasamy Deveraj (Madras, India, 1994); "The Firewalkers," "Nineteenth-Century Rain," "Northern Lights," and "Moss" in *Nineteenth-Century Rain* (Whistle Press, 1994); "Saturday Night Two-Step" in *Family: Tradition and Possibility*, ed. Jim Villani (Pig Iron Press, 1995); and "The Boys Have Guns" in *The XY Files: The Truth about Men* (Sherman Asher Publishing, 1996).

My gratitude to the Ucross Foundation and the Virginia Center for the Creative Arts for time, space, and support that allowed some of the poems in this collection to be written, and special thanks to Arthur and Janet Brennan, the wonderful publishing team at Casa de Snapdragon, who bring insight, patience, and enthusiasm to everything they do.

Contents

Book One

At Browning's Pond

Breakfast at the Lake

Quiet River

Book Two

Nineteenth-Century Rain

Flood Tide

Book Three

The surface of the water was covered by warm and different shades of gold and looked like a bed of autumn leaves gently moved by the wind. It's hard to say exactly how many there were, but in the range of a few thousand. We were surrounded by them without seeing the edge of the school and we could see many under the water surface too.

— Sandra Critelli
From the photo series, *"Golden Rays of Mexico"*

All water has a perfect memory and is forever trying to get back to where it was.

— Toni Morrison

Book One

At Browning's Pond

Loon Hunting on Newry Mountain

The first morning we discovered our limits:
the trail up the mountain buckled,
then broke under us
like a wave.

In the green valleys gray mist caught on twigs,
on boulders: thralls to gravity, we prayed
for the ease we missed.

The ascent glittered with mica —
glassy muscovite layered in dogeared "books"
and lepidolite, lavender, but smelling of time
not lilacs — and watermelon tourmaline
teased us into eating rock.

We learned that water wore no pinions
but swiftness and, under the light strength of white pine,
translucence: always deceitful, promising clairvoyance
at each arabesque and ripple.

Before the summit — fireweed, freeholder and healer,
riffling its magenta garment.

Our heads floated over the peak, torso-
less, heard the loon's high-throated laughter,
saw that black neck periscoping
beneath red oak, gold water:

a green soul flying through leafless silence.

Charles Adés Fishman

Northern Lights

I.
Walk down from the cottage — the trees
await you: wooden bridges over the swales.
In 1937, some wizard was ready to put a trailer park
here. At night, walk in again, under the frost-light
of the stars: billions of glittering branches
weaving the forest sky, the canopy
where you are married again to the universe.

II.
Once you saw the northern lights up here.
You sat on the earth, in darkness, the second-
hand of your lives silently sweeping. Wind sang
in the trees   on the beach, the black waves tumbled.
This boreal realm — here, you would embrace again
the dark flame of your love: in this virgin timber,
you were a fire that would not be concealed.

III.
You walk these woods all day, get lost in them
— comfort and peace tramping the underbrush
before darkness descends. Even at noon, the tide
of sunlight is held back by thick foliage, the over-
lap of leaves, the heavy curtain of balsam: only
little rays cut through here, ghosts of light,
rounds and circlets, a spreading fan of spirits.

At Browning's Pond

I doubt now I could find it:
the map is erased in that corner,
paved over.

Once I played there, late in a warm
October. I think I was nine.
Blackbirds cried out in the cattails.

My mind was a swamp of feelings:
soft black mud, standing water.
I waded through reeds and leeches,
splashed with a pickerel's ease.

This, too, is a gate I must open:
still pond, the sun that lingered,
redwing of my heart. Water
that pours now through my fists,
water that calms and pleases.

That day, I swam with the glint
of a shiner right off the map
of childhood.

The pond was a mystery almost as deep
as my body.

Far into Vermont

1.
In the cup of mountains
silence is black China tea
the spirit drinks. Coyote screams
welcome moonlight risen
above the gap in the black
porcelain hills.

This is what stillness is for:
to bring peace to dust,
to teach bones quiet.

Shadows exist without people
and darkness is surf come too near.
A hand is no match for the sugary flesh
of blueberries.

Here it is darker than the inside
of your mouth. Hummingbird sips
from each star.

2.
Lichen on tree (old storm-
blasted maple), moss on granite
boulder, gradations of green
on the Green Mountains: green
dark as hemlock in black December,
rust-red greenness of first frost,
rolling Vermont meadow   cleared field
birchwood   and twisted crabapple   coolness
in the smart breeze that knows solitude,
salutes it: every shadow here is the imprint
of something living, even the moss-and-lichen-
covered rock that roots down to the core
of the begotten planet.

Moss

One day soon, the earth
will be covered by moss,
by gray and yellow lichen,
by spreading fans of fern.

Here, too, rooftops
are warped and green —
peaked rectangular bogs.

* * *

I saw a cave opening
and wanted to climb in,
but the walls sloped obliquely,
dripping gold and indigo flowers:

a nearly vertical planet
orbiting a dead sun,
a drizzling emptiness.

I saw the stones glimmer
in that green kingdom
and bridges garnished with vines,
green veins simmering
in the earth's succulent body.

* * *

The path went deeper,
bending back on itself, but still winding quietly   perilously
upwards.

The earth was trammeled with life —
forever tendriling.
I could feel the toe-taps on my neck, white rootlets,
that itchy lushness gaining
a freehold.

* * *

Light laid its spectral eggs on my forehead, on my green
and sprouting shoulders.

Charles Adés Fishman

Whapmagoostui

Hydro-Québec in James Bay Wilderness, 1992

A silence wells up at the mouth
of the river, north of Québec,
in the haunted light of a culture . . .
silence deep as the bay, burden
of many rivers: Eastmain and Moose,
Nottaway and Attawapiskat, the La Grande
and this, that rolls and flashes
beneath us, *Whapmagoostui*, the Great
Whale. Miles of dark-green black spruce
and white spruce, taller, ash-barked, dress
the guardian hills. Here, millennia
of ponds have glittered in first light,
translucent as blown glass or turbid, hue-
shifting, like molten pewter; lakes polished
smooth in the near-Arctic sun: trays of native
silver; rivers swollen with pike, whitefish, salmon;
geese in the rippled streams, snowy owls in darkening
branches; caribou chesting the current; endless
tide of blood, meat, hide, horn, bone, music.

After sundown, a red hunter's moon rises
over the stalking grounds of the Cree nation.
Lodges are fragrant with elk skins, with evergreen
boughs. The night is bisected, then quartered,
by shimmering light that spangles the black dream
of hills. Water burns with the light.

For five thousand years, the people sat around this fire:
chanted, gave thanks, grieved, laughed and remembered.
Ancestors are buried here.

A cry spirals up like the rasp of a red-tailed hawk.

Ice Music

Where the paired swans feed
and row the lake to softness,
two boys toss stones at the ice.
One week to Solstice, they throw
their arms out, angling for that other shore
where the lake is still unfrozen.
They hope some chancy sequence
of skitters and leaps will serve them.
Keepers of mystery, they reach for a small island
it is far too soon to walk to. Cracking shadow-ice,
they fracture harmony: ear-splitting chirps
and trills and tremolo silences. Listen:
it is the bird of sheer delight   warbling to winter.

July 1946

That summer trees talked: a whisper
I still hear. The farmer's collie
sprawls on the front steps, the cottage
is white and calm, a wooden ship snugly
anchored. This is the day I sail
out of reach, light as a dandelion puff,
a forked seed floating.

What will I find in the shade of the dark
trees, hidden among the branches? a name
like a nest to sleep in? a name black
as the chanting leaves? I know this
stillness. Once before I was warmed
like this, nourished directly.

This is the day I am here, the breath
of centuries rushing through me,
the mouths of my blood speaking . . .
Ahead, where the road bends, no one
comes for me, not even that good golden
dog, that cottage door into early morning,
my mother in her housedress of scarlet flowers,

murmuring the day's first meal.

Charles Adés Fishman

On the Spirit Pipes

Pitlochry, Scotland
June 19 —

This is where the train stops
and my spirit lightens, even as darkness
falls — such exceeding slowness! —
and night comes on. In the shallow Tummel
where the Grampians run black ripples
toward Inverness, salmon still lunge
and the late sky, pearl and charcoal now,
holds white at the bleached horizon.

If you were to leave this place
and walk carefully, winding down
the rough-edged road that cuts
through town, along the narrow footpath,
to the fish ladders at Pitlochry Dam,
from there along the black silk of river,
and over the river on the one swaying, heart-trembling
bridge, all the harsh cold beauty
of the country, its wild and still-present history,
would flow into you.

Breakfast at the Lake

Romance

We meet near the water,
mid-December: clear day
but cold by the pond
iced over at the lip.
This is our first time,
so I keep my hood down —
you deserve a face.

I arrive early, walk
the pond's rim, past
the old mill whose wheel
won't turn, swings frozen
in summer. Geese inspect me . . .
I admire their savage beaks.

Mallards paddle the gray-black water,
cluster at the edge. The males
have green heads that shine
— all except this one: at the brink,
he lifts high his crown, its satin sheen
blue as peacock feathers. He is the duck

I would save from predators,
from death in the ice. That blue head
dreams in a different universe,
like your streaked blonde one.
Something reaches from me
to shelter you, to gather you
from the cold, the wind
breaking the rushes.

15

The Dream

When you appeared in my dream
with your eyes blackened,
I knew it was a sign.

I knew I had understood
the secret of your illness,
your sudden collapse, your screams
and doubled-over frailty,
your youthful face blotted, only
a pale drained mask in its place.

I knew my own body was as vulnerable,
that what we call *getting older*
is really an uncovering,
the delicate inner shell revealed.

This thought drove the life
from me, and I joined you on the bed
where you rested, my life companion.
And I held you in my sudden weakness,
clinging to your bare legs and your
narrow back, breathing your warm neck
and your hair.
                    It was then,
at our closest — our weakest —
I knew nothing less than death
could break us, that death wouldn't
break us.

Breakfast at the Lake

Don't you love good food and plenty
of time to eat it — no clock to tick
the mouthfuls? That, and you near me,
healing.

The fire crackles down to its last
embers. The lake is still — not frozen
but held quiet by the steady hand
of January. You could drink in that quiet
for a century   and not be filled.

There! The flames rise again
of themselves: a moment out of childhood
when you still believed, the room —
gone dark and shadowy — suddenly bright
again, a dream you've waked from and are
now living.

Don't you love it, the way each forkful
eases you into morning? Months
we raced the clock, tempers hot
and flaring. And now, this food —
fried egg folded over mushrooms,
sweet peppers —

the fragrance of onion and fresh dill
soothing you again   salvaging something
that had seemed lost.

Charles Adés Fishman

January 1991

Snow doesn't fall — it blows down
through branches, ice-tipped
and feathery, blows sideways
under eaves. Out into the untracked
main street, snow-soft, we walk, old lovers
still young, life's rushing brook still quick in us.
As always, it is good to walk out of this world
with you, to turn into two silvery flames.
For a time, everything is laid smooth again,
eider down sift of mid-winter . . .
Your bootprints in the snow are tentative
as deer tracks, mine long scuffed snowshoe flags.
The storm steers toward the coast, but snow
comes heavily now, blowing your life
more deeply into my own.

A Small Fire

The flames were teal blue
with pale orange crowns.
On the radio, Garth Brooks
was crooning a country/western tune.
Jodie let the rack of lamb cook
in its juices   sat back for a while
sipping a deep red wine — a burgundy
or merlot — something dark and bright
at once.

El, too, allowed the strings
to go slack. It was good to see her
ease her legs up   to watch her open
the top button at her throat.
How good to see the music enter her,
to sense the rich aromas dreaming
into her blood. Even Mark had settled back
now, letting the sweet pungency
calm him: such a fine host, a brother
to admire and love.

More orange in the dancing flames,
the blue ghosts holding to center.
In that moment, the future unfolded
its petals of ice and fire. *Young love!*
sang the Judds, *Strong love! True love!*
and the fire shot up: a small fountain
of blue and orange flames.

Flying

We walk deep into the sea's planet.
Egrets fly over, flaunting their stylish black feet
— *à la mode* in the salt marsh.

Merlins and sparrowhawks plunge into trees
beneath the highest branches. Mergansers and grebes
flush from the breaks at each step.

Our softest whisper scatters songbirds.

* * *

Today the sun came back and called us: out of our rainy
nights and painfully bright rooms, called us
to this beachy wood, all the trees on fire with autumn,
grasses webbed with seeds. Here we can be free —
the ordinary world turned over — for a while, no trespass.

* * *

By this gently pulsing water, lie back and dream.
Goldenrod seethes like a storm-cloud of butterflies,
and blue sky drifts, defining and deepening perfection.

Held aloft by pleasure, we float effortlessly, monarchs
of all we obey.

Charlotte Amalie: Three Passions

I. *Noon*
My forty-eighth year wakens to rain and sunlight.
The day grows brighter. At high noon, I climb
in tropic heat to the old Sephardic temple —
with you, again, my wife.

We like the feel of consecrated ground,
though we need no priest or rabbi. Our vows
hold fast: hard work and undiminished caring.

II. *Dusk*
Dining with you is the harbor at twilight
and nightfall over the city. You are the right wine
to complement the meal, the chef's special sauce
that draws succulence from the lamb.

Music that enters like a vine twining down a waterfall
is your presence at the table, all my days
made more pungent, headier, with you so close.

III. *Evening*
Later, the winding stair of a converted sugar mill
lures us into night's clear country. From this height,
the heart of the island opens up, light on light,
in a dazzling scatter.

Before we go, I climb the stair alone —
your holding back, the finest gift.

So May All Poems Bear Fruit

I turn to Hikmet's "The Cucumber,"
charmed by his clear eye and clearer spirit
but, halfway through the Moscow snow,
bathed by the green sun of his words,
I remember the cucumber I picked for you today
— young, tender, hidden beneath the trellis
of spatulate leaves. It was a firm, completed thing
yet, underneath, yellow-white from lack of sun,
and I placed it on a river rock in my flower bed
like a half-green message to the stars:
I set it there to soak in the day's heaviest light,
so it might drink deeply and perfect itself —
that greenness might favor it entirely —
and it was only here, as I leafed through
Hikmet's poems, that I was brought back
to the still fruit awaiting my attention: your gift
forgotten this summer afternoon, forgotten
and now remembered.

Mother of Silence

Rain on the sea, in sunlight, or
memory of rain, memory of sea,
memory of light: sun on each patchy
wave, each swatch of wake green
as a camouflage jacket, but translucent,
the white silk of crushed shells distant, muted,
an *underness*.

Enter this rain of ions, photons of tide
and body, your eyes darkly glimmering
in the dark trough   in the plosive burr
of ocean: your eyes and their sadness, wife,
your deep sadness, and your love: for me,
for our children, for the children
of children —

Even in this stark sun, your eyes
bring fresh rain to my spirit: rain
that bids roses drink deeply   and bend
toward death, rain to wash daisies white
as new snow: rain on the sea and on the earth,
rain that cossets and cleanses, rain that quenches,
that quiets the nerves   of the planet.

Quiet River

Shanti

The dog comes into view, swimming
strongly, the thrown stick in her mouth.
In the pearly morning light, her left front leg
can be seen working beneath the pale jade surface.

She is so black, her coat so dense and silky,
the light can never fully find her, for she is
a black cloud that has settled on the snow   an oil
slick with ears and paws that clings to coastal rocks.

In a field of fallen leaves, she is the burnt stump
of cottonwood or oak that puts out a six-inch bud
of pinkest tongue.

                    * * *

Fortunate dog, to be given these spaces,
to be always loved, central to the season.
Someone who had no childhood asks that you walk
beside her, that you run free   but come back,

faithfully. Later, when sickness is a thick new rope
that won't slip from your master's hand, she
lies down beside you and keeps you warm. But,
finally, your death can't be put off.

There is no lid to the body leaking out your life.

                    * * *

Charles Adés Fishman

Here is what she wants: that you might live
inside her, apostle of the senses, transmitter
of joy and peace. And so she wrenches open her mouth
and barks the words that heal you of your pain.

She carries the dust of you back to the earth
you loved, the leaf-dazed autumn woods of Door
County. She buys candles and sets their wicks aglow
and lies down where you slept to speak your name —

she whimpers it: the name is a leash
that won't let go.

Near Crazy Woman Canyon

Deep into the canyon carved slowly
by the river, immense boulders have crashed
down from the cliffs: sheer red-gold
and black-blazed rock.

The rock, the river, excite,
but the grass ocean beyond them calms.
In the soft wheat and washed-gold
of the fields, the mind grows quiet.

It is good to soak up the sky,
to let your blood dream of the shale-green waters
of a distant lake. Even sun-dulled silver wire, strung
in four strands to mark off boundaries,

seems part of the natural landscape. Humanity's
tragic song is distant as the unseen stars,
but the breeze of existence is a whisper
in your ear, the soft choral hush

of a hidden waterfall. Prairie cone flowers
by a fence and silver grass in the meadow
and the orange-gold of the fields: motherland
is here.

Charles Adés Fishman

In the Path of Lightning

I. Bobby

Laura, his mother, had died
from the white lightning
of alcohol: eight months back
she had sunk down into a black
delirium, had reached out to him

from the bed where she writhed,
where she raved in her poisoned
idiom. From the twisted, piss-
stained sheets, she had called to him —
had seemed to — so that his fear

of abandonment had eased, the slip-
knot tightened around his heart
had loosened.

Eight months Laura was in the grave
when Bobby visited her. He knelt
to place the flowers she had loved
when awake and sober: black-eyed
Susan, sprays of bergamot and chicory.

He remembered how she would hold
the fragile bright bouquet, crushing it
to her breast; always, a few blooms
would break, a flurry of petals fall: droplets
of blue and violet and ingot-yellow.

The room would open then, brushed
with those quiet odors; the house would feel safe.
This is what he remembered — this undersong
beneath his pain — but Laura was in her grave
and he would not be comforted.

The storm that blew up, just as he rose
and turned, had wrestled him back to his knees:
he could not take leave of her. His mother —
how clearly he could see her in the first klieg-
flash of lightning! how the pines had shrieked

in that turbulence, so like his mother
when she lived. He ran, then, from what he
kept of her   and could not escape. This
was the burst fury of her life. It was his.

II. Laura

She had been blond once, a girl
of fifteen, slender, adventurous —
but life had shown her how the planet
could unwind, the street beneath her window
buckle . . . how a father could turn into a fox,

a weasel, an eagle, a wild dog. And death
had etched her mother's face, had lifted the mask
on sorrow, filling that broken house with brute
anger, with a graveyard of guilty silence.

* * *

In the drink-blurred life that followed,
she had found her husband, Richard.
He was so like her father when she first
laid eyes on him, he was already drunk,
but he'd made her think of home. Someday,

she'd have a home again: husband, children —
perhaps one child, a son, who would forgive
her memories with his own. She had. She *did*.
But voices from her childhood had mocked her,
had left her mute, and hard liquor had quickly

shut her down and carried her toward darkness.
Her son had stood by her to the last — to the last
drumbeat, the last nagging whine of the clarinet.

When he appeared that day, eight months later,
she couldn't keep back her anger or her love:
the storm was hers — thunder that crashed viciously
down, a spike of blue lightning that split
a sheltering pine, and that tantrum of elemental fire

that had spared Bobby but scorched her husband's heart.

III. <u>Richard</u>

The lightning had been meant for him
for, even in death, she felt it: that tortured
rivalry neither of them could win. The bolt
she'd sent him had known his name: would mark him.
Hadn't he done the same — knife flash or knuckles —

a thousand times: some reckless slash at fate, destiny,
chance that had made him, once, seem strong?
Yet she had not meant to kill him with that wild kiss
of electrons — only to wake him from his long
violent sleep.

Alive, she'd had no way to fight him: When he
steamed up on that Harley, the air had hushed
around him. And he'd been lean, tall, tattooed:
tanned in that burnt-blond leather-and-fire way
of every hardrock biker. And she had loved the road:

so many green and sun-doomed miles. For a time,
under that one full moon of the universe, she'd been
his queen and bride. *Yes.* But what if it had been only
his angry beauty she had loved, his arrogance —
that certainty he had that life existed only

where he was?

Raymond Martin

He was born and raised a Virginian,
an old country boy who knew
every notch and hollow, had fished
every stream. Each bordered field
in that sweet Southern land
had taken up residence in his heart
where there were no boundaries.

It was why he'd walked Virginia's
rich cadastral map that took on
more detail as the swift years passed.
He knew each bluff and byway,
each culvert and creek where the history
of this nation changed, where change
had been written in blood.

Virginia was his country, and he
could name each tributary and tidewater
village, every burial ground and Civil War
campaign. Her rivers were poetry to him —
the Mattaponi   Rappahannock   Chickahominy —
and, if he could, he'd have rafted the sky
over Richmond, Roanoke, Alexandria.

He remembers fifty, sixty, years ago, the fine
hachures of families, the hard good lives
of friends, and his three dark years
in the Great War that forever marred
the world. He remembers, though he's
getting old and the map has grown un-
recognizable: each bypass, interchange,

strip mall   alters history. Just ask Raymond.
He once walked each county and, given time,
could still name them. To live a century
is a kind of vindication, and the names
of the dead swim back: choruses of praise
and devotion and a country boy's long dirge
of grief. How deeply he's loved Virginia.

Quiet River

A family of wigeons in shadow —
When the female turns her beak skyward,
she knows what I am, cries out to her little ones,
then heads straight downstream:
staccato arrowing swim.

I know her tactic, the history that guides her,
yet my eye follows her retreat and I almost miss
the silent, graceful escape
her quintet of ducklings makes:
dusky, obedient creatures,
they climb the bank and fade, then dissolve
and vanish, as she rows the long way back.

* * *

Life is the river's song: in the deep drops
and silted shallows, ripples and slashes
of song, small explosions of melody
as a trout's face breaks the surface.

The river bottom is a *raga* of black stones, white stones
the size of human feet, thigh bones of beige rock
and magenta. On the surface, pale white florets:
dull lights in dark water.

* * *

Upstream, the water churns, disturbed babble
of moments. In jazz riffs of feeder streams
and tributaries sluicing from the hills, its music
brightens: cross-hatched and slashing, the river furls
in small waves, in fish-spine ripples.

Downstream, where tall grasses cling, mirrored
and softened, the current runs smooth
as cooled lava.

* * *

An elbow of river: grasses parched the dour color
of deer skulls   a siege of sienna and red-violet   streamers
steeped in mustard and jade   a trumpet-burst
of gold-yellow blooms.

The river forks here and, in noon light, appears azure,
barred with white and Prussian, like an old dream
of jays.

* * *

Cows have come down to the river.
Still, almost sculpted into the landscape,
they graze in slow, assiduous motion:
this slope of the mountain is range land they know.
The late morning haze of high Wyoming summer,
its rich mix of oils and drifting pollens,
weave a zone of safety around the herd.

* * *

In the brush: twinned sulfur butterflies, black-
and-yellow-striped grasshoppers, dragonflies cruising
thick August air. Wild oats in the musky breeze
and cheat grass with its pendant spikelets,
green tufts of bristlegrass, foxtail barley spreading red
and champagne fans.

* * *

After last night's storm, the lightning-flashed hills
and splashed-down torrents, the country seems stilled,
the current placid, as if the land itself has been quieted.

On the far bank, a great blue heron: its long white-
and black-mottled bill aimed at the river,
the plane of its folded wing a blue-gray swatch
of rain cloud.

* * *

Wind scuffles leaves of the cottonwoods.
On the path near the river butterflies linger:
the breeze, cooling now, hurries them along
yet, in a field of beebalm and timothy,
a white or pale yellow patch clings
to each violet flower.

In a spill of still water and reeds, the river
shushes but, a few feet away, it is silver-brushed
under the rasp of the wind.

* * *

Incessant clatter of grasshopper wings
in the sea of drying stalks: when they gust up
against my chest, a blizzard of crisp gray bodies,
it is as if a deaf heart outside me
has started beating.

Wyoming Nights

1.
Wind brushes through, buffs fields
to a green shine. Dense gray and pink-
fledged clouds blossom and drip time's
thick honey at the edges of the planet
where evening chimes down and blue-
frocked barn swallows dive and cry out.
Above dun and dusk-green hills, the first
full August moon of creation lifts its pink-
orange face to the world. Night blackens
and lightens at once, driving space deeper
into being and pulling down shadow
and memory from under the eaves of the stars.
In gullies and shallow dips in the fenced-off
meadows, water spangles and, over rock crests,
a rim of blazing light flares up, then dies.
Black night ascends from the roots of trees,
seeps up from wet and silent fields, dreams itself
all distance and desire.

2.
Campfire at night, the sky behind it smoking . . .
Sparks break free of the seething and smoldering wood.
In darkness beyond the fire, the half-orange moon
holds still above a black grove of trees.

The starred sky remembers old signs and omens: hero,
huntsman, goddess, lion, swan, and we pull back
from the fire, stare, growing quieter: we know this dream
beyond the flames, this tarrying at the edge of breath —

Death-still our watch, but the fire is fluid, blue-tipped,
ceaseless, and alive. It builds a cindery Eden
for our senses, warms us   and then chills.

And we who linger here will walk these coals
in a trance of waiting, will float with the night wind
above Wyoming, journeyers at the beginning.

3. *Medicine Wheel Vision*

The wheel is a wreck of stones:
twenty-eight spokes enclosed in barbed wire.
The stones were assembled here
seventeen centuries ago. The sea of night
is full.

The seeker is not ready. He has been
to the sweat lodge, has breathed
the cleansing heat, but he is not ready.
There is no light in his body. He will go
to the mountain.

The wheel is ten thousand feet up, near
to the wind and stars, near to the eagle's
hearth, the lair of coyote, the harrier's nest.
Like the seeker, it waits: this place
is not for tarrying.

* * *

At Solstice, the light of the sun
strikes the wheel . . . the first spoke
is on fire. His nights are given to fasting,

waiting: Elk is a sign, White Crow is a sign.
Feathers catch the wind of half a billion years

At night, his songs warm him. In a cairn
of stones, he has waited . . . *A light comes on
in his body.* Arapaho, Lakota, Shoshone, Sioux:
The courage of his tribe has spoken to him.

Bear and Elk have spoken to him.
Ice and Lightning have spoken to him.
A light comes on in his body. The night heron cries
over dark water.

4.
Perfect weather until
the Perseids — luminous blue
skies — but, tonight, sheet lightning
over the mountains . . .

Animals live in this night:
young deer by the river at twilight
as the storm breaks in the west
and comes closer: jags and flashes
of lightning. A chestnut bay
in a battered corral near the highway
whinnies into dance, settles when
I speak to him. Lightning strikes
the hills, bites the river, swipes
at earth and sky — and rain
sweeps over us, horse, deer, and man,
fills ditches and rain barrels,
then races off.

The storm lingers over the Bighorns:
shifting white flashes like an aerial
bombardment, but here it is clear again:
overhead, the dog star, Rigel,
and the unnamed dark.

5.
The storm comes back. A soft drizzle
of rain, then a flash that scalds,
that proves the vulnerability
of the body: the universe afire,
then set on fire again.

6. *Night Driving*

The road is crushed red shale
and skirts the edge of the mountain,
unwinding as it goes. No one but you
is on it and you're moving along
with the wind, watching mile markers
stitch white patches into the horizon.

You push the gas pedal down
and the wheels respond: wherever
you're headed, you'll get there soon.
This is the freedom you've craved,
the space not to be found at home,
and you want to hoot and holler
with the joy of speed, with the power
that shoots through your body.

* * *

Then the deer's in front of you
and there's no time to stop,
though you're braking hard enough
to halt the spin of the planet.
Her blood smears the smashed-in hood,
the busted headlamp, and her body
lies there in the road, gathering
all the light.

7. *Late August*

Near the river at night, a deer
and her fawn cross the road, vanish
in the field. A cool breeze blows
under the summer stars. In the cattails
and under the cottonwoods, the river
is a dark rush of blood.

8. *Starlight*

I go out into the night. The stars
are alive in their death-silences, they
speak: our blood knows this dialect.
It is still summer, but the chill of winter
has licked the air: the crisp edge of starlight
on the grass in the field.

The heart feels this cool breath of space,
this whisper of the death of all things,
and it throbs louder, it wants to be this light
that floods down at it from the past,
it wants no part of death, it wants and it wants . . .

And you, too, breathe in the path of this light,
this sweet deep unnamable fragrance that bathes us now,
that showers us with existence.

Book Two

Nineteenth-Century Rain

Nineteenth-Century Rain

If we can't have the kudu's mask and the bell
shaped like a nursing mother and the amulet,
a miniaturized human head; if not the blood-rite
and dawn-quiet of the hunter; then let us have
nineteenth-century rain.

Allow us the forgiving sun in Inness' *naïve* "Sunset"
that soothes as it breathes out fire; allow us
the luminous still landscape, deeps of forest
not yet given to the saw.

* * *

In John Stanley's "Mount Hood," trees and boulders
are central: this barely settled shore seems unreal,
astonishingly whole —a trope for all we have vanished
in our century.

O native, under-utilized, America, your tribe of priests
in the foreground, earth-red tipis crouched at the verge
of pale yellow and aqua water: this could be the West's
Nile Valley. *Let us not climb the white pyramid!*

* * *

Let us grow silent as turquoise. If not the cleft skull
of the mountain, then a skull-cap of white wool;
if not the death-mask of the python, then the unpeopled
plain, the black night of the Salampasu.

Allow us wildflower heartlands, fish leaping in creeks,
blessing of fresh deep snow, leaf-filtered sunlight, sweet
timeless rain. For us, the visionary landscape, not sun-
bleached bone, cemetery of spines and antlers.

The Firewalkers

Lankadas, Greece, 19 —

Like his mother before him,
he is the chief firewalker.
All year, he has meditated, fasted,
prayed; he has walked in the scorched shoes
of a dream. He's done the god-work
of the village, waiting for that blinding moment
when the flames might seize him
and draw him near.

Forty years ago, exactly, his mother
walked the coals at Kosti, under
a Thracian sky: barefoot like him,
adored by the flames   like him.
She knew the truth songs, her heart
was on fire like his. In her arms,
she had held the secret — the flames
were obedient to her saints.

This late spring morning, Kyriakos,
the gardener, has put the bull to the knife;
its black pelt gleams in the slant rays
of the sun. The day is hot, the light glaring.
The stripped flesh of olive trees smolders.
Sotirios has watched: his prayers, his singing,
have come to this. His hunger has come to this.
All will be ready when darkness falls
and fire finds its home.

Greece from Above

On older roofs, the deep orange
has rubbed off   eroded now
to pale tones of old pottery,
a few stained and bleached bones.

Like soldiers who survived the War
of Independence, roof tiles exhibit
their wounds   the deep scars
of rust   the black fever of weather.

In the distance, every hue vanishes
into mauve but, in local dominion,
history remains: the blue dome
of a church niched in the highest

quarter   a child's cry flashing
its white wing-bars   the foaming
green tide breaking where the hills
have burned   above the ruins of Athens.

Road with Cypress and Star

— van Gogh, May 1890

Earlier, the trees are earth,
then water and flame — but here
they are smoke, dark green smoke
. . . turrets of blue wind.
As always, what we thought
complete, *frozen*, seethes
with contradictory fires.
Reeds sweep diagonally across
this landscape, not orange
but ochre, and their heart's blood
is change. They will shake
the cottage, dreaming in its copse
of cypresses — will *lean*, breathing
fine showers of light. Even the sky
is a sea that splashes and burns,
and the stars that swim in this ripeness
are living creatures: two stars,
and the moon's startled mouth,
and this river of transluminous
pigment, this blackgreen pyre
of cypresses. Here, all is desire,
and these nearly human figures . . .
flesh that will not be consumed.

Charles Adés Fishman

Listening to Brahms

a forest is laid waste. Birds sing
to each other, shaming the violins.
Rain drifts down in shadow
torn from the farthest sky. Listening
to Brahms, the oceans prepare to die
and black tsunamis hurry toward the land.
Cities darken, the membrane over the earth's core
parts. We are listening to Brahms: the nineteenth
century taunts us. In the Sahel, the dead pile up.
Sand gushes like oil from the mouths of the Sahara.
On Sinai, Silence speaks in shrouds. Rain falls
with the ghost-arms of the forgotten. The orchestra
of birds plays on. Listening to Brahms, the percussionist
awaits his moment. It is Brahms who shatters the bow,
who makes the severed strings of the closing millennium
vibrate.

A Spanish Nocturne

1.
In the back alley that gathers all things
from the *Gran Via,* light
shuts down
                    and voices come up
the way a symphony discovers itself
in the hands of a great conductor.

2.
A lone man in white cloth
sloshes the street with buckets
of black water.

3.
Songs of the Gypsies whisper
on the hill of Sacromonte.

Charles Adés Fishman

At Yeats's Grave

We went to Sligo over narrow roads
eroded at the edges by rain.
We wanted to see the country
that had startled Yeats into song:
the waters of Lough Gill and Glencar Lake.

We wanted to see the grave
of Ireland's greatest poet—how it waits
by his grandfather's church at Drumcliffe
with its taut verse and gray stillness
how Ben Bulben's battered face
floats beyond it in the verdant sea
of a late May morning.

We wanted to walk where Yeats
had stitched his lines   and unstitched them
where he had known defeat in each ripped stanza
and victory in the rise and fall of each imperfect
syllable. We would walk with him
where history had beaten down
like sudden gusts of rain.

We would walk where Yeats had walked
and listen for the wingbeats of Irish poetry.
By then, the Sligo sun could be shining
and *peace* might sound as sweet
as church bells on Sunday morning.

Old Man with Cane Looking out Train Window

Sunlight finds his combed-back hair.
He has the elongated ear of the old, the high
ridged forehead, large mottled hands.
When, for a train stop, the late October sun
seems earth-bent on testing him, he leans
his strong head back: this, the head for a coin!
His metal cane stands with its curved hand-hold
gripped now in both meaty palms, then one palm,
the other partly clouding his face. His dark blue
waist-length jacket open, he is handsome still,
though steadily the bones weaken, the body sinks
into its shell. The window is familiar, patient
as his cuffed brown slacks, comfortable as the crepe-
sole shoes. Glint of sunshine in leaves that have
not yet fallen, white-steepled village church, flag
that blares its overkill of stars: so much takes him back!
Home is near — house roof, sidewalk, bridge, and lake.
All of this floods in and will not grant him rest.

Charles Adés Fishman

A Shade from "Glory"

Charlottesville, 19—

As credits rolled, the bit player strode
out of the wings, still dressed in Union-blue.
"Any questions?" he asked. His audience —
late twentieth-century brew of red-clay Confederates,
Virginia regulars, Yankees light-years from home —
froze: ultra-slow motion.

This was the real thing, wasn't it? the outrider
who'd come for us. If we didn't reach automatically
for rifles or jackets, didn't charge the exits,
didn't string him up or chain him down —
it was certain the others would follow:
the good white soldiers, spruce in gray or blue,

bayonets ready, taking the gleam of the sun —
they would come, right foot, left foot, legions! down;
and the bad white soldiers, they'd come, too,
swearing, bantering — battle-scarred elders,
the brutally young; and the brave dead soldiers,
black in the theatre's dark —

those who fought nobly and were blown apart,
those who lived to see the war finished
but not to be won — they, too, would stand here;
and even Colonel Shaw, that death-pale boy, color-bearer
for the unfinished sequel — maybe Shaw himself
would come.

Maybe if we kept asking questions, they would all
stroll out, would fill the screen of our minds again —
screen of our hearts. And that would be *it*, wouldn't it?
Wasn't that the one question we cared to have answered:
to know, after thousands of stuttering flicks,
thousands of spliced tellings,

if real life could finally overtake us, horse unseat us,
bullet waste us, our own ghosts greet us —
to know if tragedy or triumph might embrace us,
uniform of any side grace us. In this after-light of glory,
we would wait for hours: as long as he was speaking,
we would listen.

Charles Adés Fishman

New Orleans Winter

1.
Mississippi,
I bring greetings
from the old gods:
from the cold voodoo
of the north,
this torch-song.

River, your old dukedom
simmers in chemical haze.

Crosses of black fire
shimmy
under the sign
of the fish.

Greetings to you,
seething gumbo!

2.
Rose at my ear, I fall
through a dream of cripples,
moral acrobats crawling alleys
of dead slave history.

Jazz-dazed, I sink to my thighs
in hot sauce, dark cornet riffs
pulsing brass and jasmine,
raw oyster bars and bead-ghosts
on maimed firework horses.

City, you open my mouth
and say *Drink! Here*
is my heart! Here
the best vein! and I
put my lips to the throat
that gleams in copper darkness,
my tongue on the salty skin,
the sweet milky coffee
of the breasts, the bittersweet pulp
laid open.

3.
Even in this cold, you are hot
glow, fat salamander colors:
nipple-tassel purple, DeChirico
orange and red:

a caravan of drag queens in ball
gowns, sequined limousines,
white beard of the horn man,
the sure-cure of gin.

Even in this cold, you grin
Drink this! you say, *Drink*
till you gasp awake!

4.
If the new order comes, here
is where it will enter:
this city of cool women and hot
jazz, food for the fire gods:
a jalapeño pepper
that will unpetal

63

in Jackson Square
and swallow Baton Rouge
with its sticky sepals:
a jambalaya garden teeming
with booze and sex and bad
politics.

5.
River,
you breathe on my neck
your last mouthful of catfish.

A Great Silence Has Descended

After Peter Matthiessen's **African Silences**

In Senegal, the land shimmers
in the hot breath of the *harmattan,*
high pale stalky grass burns
near every village, and the earth
is black. In Gambia, bamboo
the brown color of burning white paper
sprouts from a crust of stone.
Everywhere, dead villages, waste-
land, emptiness. Later, under
the stars, an enormous burning tree
of the doomed African forest.

Then the forest opens, the bank
of a river rises up to meet us, travelers
in the late twentieth century of death:
a flute, melodious and wistful, high
and unceasing, sings out, dance
of the forest ghosts. At Ouazamon,
small stone hearths, gourd calabashes
of shining bronze, long wooden ladles
and stone pestles laid out on the swept earth
like ancient art. At the forest edge,
birds: dark hornbills, red-eyed doves, pygmy
kingfishers, cattle egrets like effigies
of carved snow. Behind them, the dark smoke
of a fire.

* * *

Zaire: pretty graveyard in a grove
of tall mimosas   hibiscus in bloom:
a dark, sinister lavender   sunlit sun-
bird on a bare limb. Tambourine doves hurl
their sad falling notes   then Lualaba,
the Congo: green as a blood-green sea, green
as the beak of a parrot god. The silver
limbs of a dead tree across the Dungu
are decked with a winged red inflorescence.
In the late twentieth century, the scars
of slavery glow in every clearing, the smell
of urine, death, anger, tyranny, and decay
drift like a mist over the green and the arid
lands. In the C.A.R., an emperor orders
the murder of thirty thousand elephants
by helicopter gunship   for the sickness
of deposed kings and their impotent admirers
the white and the black rhino are butchered
and de-horned   the bush elephant is coaxed
toward extinction with buzz saws and AK-47s.

In the Congo Basin, a great silence has descended,
but a sudden burst of reedbuck out of a thicket
in the grassy swale and the heart leaps again —
like a male diadem butterfly with big white dots
on black wings, it flutters back to life.

* * *

Ever more quietly, we move into the rain forest.
The dust of the world swirls in cathedral light
in long sun shafts and, high overhead,
a bright *mbolo* fruit swells with sun in a chink
of blue sky. Here, a white pilot in a military aircraft
armed with firebombs and rockets gunned down a troop
of elephants. The nightjars warned, but Angola,
with her Cuban mercenaries, financed guerrilla war
with the sale of ivory from a hundred thousand dead.

And so we fly over the burned and ruined
plateaus of the Congo Republic into a killing storm.

* * *

The once green continent of Africa struggles
in its sleep, chained to old ways and new
terrors, a tethered cockerel whose bill gapes
with fear and thirst. In the soft murmuring
of fire and smoke, in the roar of animal
slaughter, it turns to the east, to the west,
but strangles on its cord. The forest knows —
the forest is — this song.

Flood Tide

Two Boys at the Seashore

They live in a desert of strangeness,
step lively on a strung wire of dreams
that sways dangerously above the seabrine.
Like firewalkers, they cross where only faith
can navigate. Ignorant of lethal winds,
tsunamis; gawky, white-blond, and nearly
hairless; their boxer swim trunks are all
that distinguish them from figures
drawn in sand.
                        A sudden gust
off the wave crests is reason to run:
quick quick quick quick quick — sandpipers.
A shadow at the shoreline is where-to-dig:
dark, wet, gritty, yielding, without
bottom. Sand is to scatter, not to protect,
and energy is what grows luminous
on their bodies: sheen over burned skin,
aura over pallor.
                        They mine the beach
for treasure, move in a haze of friendship
and unknowing. Green trunks and red,
they disappear slowly, dissolve into purple
blackness, into seagrape air, at the horizon.
What is left are hieroglyphs: tracks
of sea ducks, sanderlings, oyster catchers,
plovers, phalaropes, turnstones —

Shadows caught in flight, let them be gathered
like shore birds wading tidepools of sun.

71

Two Girls Leaping

1.
They have a favorite color — this one:
this chlorinated aqua, this womb lunar blackness
drawn wholly into the light. The depth of the pool
beguiles them, the weight of their own bodies.

Mother is not near, so it is easy to jump in, to test
themselves against the cold liquid fire of the violently
blue water, to attempt flight, hands linked in a joyous
failure of suicide.

They wear no caps: dark hair spills black puppy tails
along their small tanned necks. Time lunges ahead, eternity
passes. A hundred leaps cannot tire them. They live
to jump: the heart of the water's coolness pulses in them.

In what way are they innocent? *The fragrance of unawareness*
stays on them: their fearful certitude about all things
perturbs the slow dark pools we swim in. In their nonstop
gab, the world's extravagant newness stings and clashes.

They are giddy with the ordinary, laugh in its cold blue
stranger's face.

2.

Becky is still laughing, gliding like a seal
in her favorite aqua water; she is giggling and splashing;
but now Mother is here, now Mother pulls her, goose-bumped
and dripping, from the ice-blue pool; now Mother slaps her,

slaps her again, again slaps her.

And Jennifer has seen everything. Watch how carefully
she moves, how cautiously she holds her tingling body.
"Let's see who can go slower," she says, "Let's see who goes
slower."

3.

The pool is empty now, a liquid rectangle. Water has its
own life, its own candor. Step back. Take a running start.
Now tell me: *What is your heart's desire?*

Charles Adés Fishman

Sand Burial

You ask me to bury you
but I want to snooze,
my thoughts stilled
for a while in a white haze,
worries not muzzled
in booze but mummied
in heat, salt spray, sea wind,
muffled by sleep. I would need
to rouse myself   to bury you.

When I wake, it is to your need.
The makeshift shovel
you hand me — a broken slat
of cast-up lumber — cuts me
from clinging tendrils.
Wound in a bedsheet,
you arrange your death scene,
your head gently supported
by the sand pillow I shape,
your body supine, wedged
against the embankment.
Lying here, with the currents
of ripe July air rushing to cover you,
you seem a species of clam, a giant bivalve
dislodged from the sea floor
and beached.

This shoveling
makes me dream: a kind of seashore
gardening. I see you are truly
a small shrub or an attached series
of tubers, sand anemone, littoral hydra.
I rake more sand onto you, bulldozing
the embankment, wanting to see you
safely entrenched at the tidemark,
wanting to watch you change:
your head feathered with beachgrass,
runic flourish of shells scalloping
your shoulders. I want to bury you deep:
corolla of white sand for your necklace,
calyx of wet seaweed for your breast,
foliage of jellyfish   at your feet.
Your sheet opens lengthwise
along the hidden seam.

Make it so I can't move — so I can't escape!

Your command wakes me and I dig faster.
I want to see you held, breathless.
The sand I bring for you now
is scooped from the waves.
I use the flat of the wood
to press that wetness
onto you. I want you
motionless, clasped
in this sea grave.
I want you emptied
of volition, entranced,
speechless, free.

* * *

There is something tender
about my movements now,
the way I brush grains of sand
from your chin, away from your nostrils
— the way I smooth your sand egg.
I want you to be covered perfectly:
a child tucked in, asleep at last
under the diligence
of my fingers.

For My Son

Spring rain has such a dark cold tongue,
yet it speaks in fire. Friend, you dreamed
I had a son — how did you know this longing,
so deeply held, that I yearned to give back gentleness
to existence, that a passion lived inside me
and held me close?

You dreamed I spoke with my son,
the two of us embracing, held fast
by some ghostly light, and you could see
from the way we leaned into each other
like two dark green flames that tendrils of rain
and lightning   reached between us.

* * *

Un-child of my blood, this life's bright reminder
that a man may nurture and reap praise, that his days
may be filled to surfeit with small pleasures —
your father blesses the muscled tautness of your body,
your powerful and steady heart.

Each year, you will love more deeply
and risk more. You will yield to the strength of others
and grow strong. Your hands will be rough
from working with the earth, fingers of iron
that arouse and soothe. You will touch
life's broken face with them.

* * *

My son, we will gaze skyward
on nights that shake us back to an age of priests
and shamans, naked and painted, alive
to the cries of the gods. The sweat of our dancing bodies
will be sweet to us, the night's fires and songs

will be sweet to us, the arms of women
will be sweet to us, the soft hair on our children's skulls
will be sweet to us. We will dance the songs,
will sing the dances. The fiery darkness will speak
to us. We will chant the names of the stars.

Icarus

He loved this girl: flames of the sun
skirled through his body. His parents warned:
there was work to be done in the dim light of morning.

But who needed sleep when a goddess called
and the night was alive with the first smells
of spring — when the black streets gleamed,

a wet gold rainbow beneath his wheels?
How could he sleep when his goddess called?
On his comet bike, he rode the world:

a hundred miles flashed by like stars,
like stars that burned inside his heart.
He was a stream of light and fire,

and she was waiting in the night,
the way the full moon waits: her touch
made vision seem less blind, her kisses

smoldered in his blood, and sleep
was banished. Who needs sleep when his soul
is called? But morning broke the night's

deep spell, and he remembered life
and woke, and he rose up from the arms
of death. The early light was azure-gold

and bathed his face in soft blue smoke.
He flew toward home, but time burned slow:
how could he sleep when sleep was death

and the night had glowed like a shooting star?

The Boys Have Guns

There must be eight of them,
no, ten, all with flashy wind-
breakers, brush cuts, scuffed
sneakers, the clean, licked
look of animals. Someone has been
mothering them, sailing them out
into this March wind to play.

The lawns they cross so casually
— clefts through enemy turf.
They speak with the cold glint
of metal, rush headlong, aimed.
Death music shoots from them.

What is it these boys hold close
to their own precious bodies?
Can it be the dark winter night
or a slain bird, still warm
and throbbing? Something soldierly
curls from their fingers like smoke.

Charles Adés Fishman

Three Boys Cycling

I wish I could have thought of them
as three boys cycling, but once their laughter
wheeled closer, circling tall trees

at our property's rim, their dark faces
were revealed, and I felt a wave surge over me
like grief   or fear. The boys were seeking help

in a strange country of neatly trimmed lawns
and white skin and they, too, were on edge.
Now that I could see them — how they held back

a little and spoke to me, then looked away —
I could tell the brave laughter I'd heard
was like a vine whose leaves had caught the light

and shined   but whose roots had been singed.
It was a long way home for them and I regretted
my meager welcome, how I'd hesitated

to fetch the tools they needed. I knew then
it was fear I felt   and not yet grief. And I could see
they sensed what I was thinking

and what held me, and I watched them waiting,
hoping I could be trusted. I think they were smarter
than me and more accustomed to being wounded,

that they knew before I did what was at stake.
And surely the boys understood that fixing the tire
wouldn't repair the situation.

Then the chore was done, the broken wheel
once again turning, a fading laughter glinting,
the golden autumn light falling.

Charles Adés Fishman

Beginning with Your Question

Where do they go, the young boys, glass
splintering their hearts? Do they drift
in melancholy fragments in tidepools
of unmown grass, or do they sift
like bits of fused brass into deeper
rifts? Where do the young boys go
who cast a spell on our hearts?
Did they die slowly into manhood:
our fathers, husbands, lovers?
our lost sons, estranged brothers?
friends no longer ripe for friendship,
broken from the vine. Where are these
scattered boys with their hands fast
on our hearts? Just yesterday, we fit
the jagged pieces together, felt the rough
edges of our existence briefly mesh . . .
Where do the young boys go, glinting, brittle
as glass? We give them our memories, our years,
and they pick the bloody splinters from our hearts.

Birthday Present

Will you surprise me or will you give me
what I want? If surprise seems in order,
please not another tie, another book, another
hair-shirt hero, another war, another liar
for president, another lost and damaged God.
Two hundred golden beetles circling
my forehead round or twelve locusts leaning
from my own right arm . . . can you arrange
such gifts? Can you cause the book of my life
to be sent, all mysteries cleared up?
or the long shelf of my lives past? Can you
give me the sky's tilt and luminosity
on the night I was born? Will you surprise me
or give me what I want? And if my desire
matters, can you give me back my trust?
the child's holy at-one-ness, unselfconscious
love? Can you put meaning back in my heart?
Will you place words in my father's mouth,
bless my mother with comprehension?
Can you present me with grandmothers?
or permit me the world as it was when to live
on this planet, this earth, was a cat's leap
from a branch — grace and clarity?

Didn't we have a contract, an honorable
agreement? I would walk in the palm
of your hand, a spirit at peace, lifted
and carried, being himself the gift.

Charles Adés Fishman

By the Sea

1.
Sea wind, you have a soft mouth
You know blessings and the mourner's *kaddish*
Ashes strewn on the waves seed the barrier beaches
                coral reefs off the Grenadines
                        atolls of Micronesia

White mouth of the black sea,
when it is time to take me do not hold back
                your power
but, until that moment, blow softly
                on me and my beloveds

Sea breeze, buttery soft in the dry heat,
                drop showers of violet sand grains
                out of this late sunlight
                            pour down on me this softening
fill my ears so the noise of this world fades
close my eyes: the inner landscape
                                will open

2.

Sea wind, blow through me
You know I am barely here, that the gull who shrieks
          his warning over my head
                    is more reliable

With your salt breath, your trance-deepened wisdom
you quiet me
                    Scoured by you, I soften

I breathe again the first smells of childhood:
          the wide ocean of my mother's body
                    smoke in my father's hair
and you, wind from the sea, bearing fresh news
                    of the planet

Your hand on me now   opens
                              my closed-off heart.

Charles Adés Fishman

Flood Tide

It rained diamonds, so I looked
to the sky. This was dazzling
and dark, both: sheaths of cloud
opening gray maroon lemon peach
turquoise. I felt my blood leap
in my body, or my body leaping.
I thought, *This is what it is
to discover flight.* I was leaning over
the parapet of myself, reaching,
straining at the bones over
my heart. Beneath me, the river
of my life brimmed with pearls
and sapphires. I was leaning over
the edge, ready to swim into the next
century. I could hear the leaves
on distant trees turn toward sudden
warmth, light breaking from the flesh,
desire synchronous with possibility.
I was who I am, and the sea and stars
knew it. Others were with me, seeking
to rise. I could gauge their power
by the flare of light that enthroned them.
Diadems rained down. Flaming arcs.
Tongues of multivalent fire.
In such company, I was free to murder
and create   and murdered death in me —
dazzling and dark, both: a rain of emeralds
and diamonds.

Book Three

Speaking Island

Cape Hatteras, 1938

I went fishing with my father
in that dream. I have the pictures
in my head: the old Woody crammed
with gear and nested in the dunes.
I have his rods, reels, sinkers,
hand-carved lures. His hip-boots
fit me snugly. This can't be memory.
For where are the striped bass
we've caught? where is the sea's
green membrane? the sea's bitter
blood? Where are the shiny scales
that should stipple our arms
and fingers? The shore tips
and heaves: stars brush our lips
with healing galactic fire. Father,
can you feel the briny stars
on your aging body? I went fishing
with you in my dream, and you reached
into the dark waves to teach me,
you walked the twilight beach with me,
you released me from my anger.
But it was death we shared, not life.
Can you feel the tide run now,
its churn and ebb? can you hear
the storm pound the sand with rain?
can you feel the line scream
in our bleeding hands? Have I hooked you,
father? Will I land your heart at last?

Charles Adés Fishman

Field

Indigo Batwing   Vermilion Goat Balls   Pineapple
Leech Soup

Father, you wouldn't speak so I collaborated
with the unspoken. I took you at your word
and kept silent   silence a field we walked
together. Your language was color and, for you,
a shade — a hue — held a full note of difference.

In this field, clear gradations of color: ragweed
pokeweed   chicory   wild carrot   nameless tufts
and over-castings of shadow: *Bronze Green,*
provocateur of exiles   Emerald Green,
that velvets the moss-lipped snow   Aquamarine,
that deepens the sea's turquoise   Cedar Green,
too dark for densities of love

In the wind's warm stillness the sun relearns
its name, gentle liftings of the scarred field
soothe the sky's broken azure. The haze
is in the seeing but the field dances: *Lemon*
Yellow, lightning after the Flood   Benzedine
Yellow, that the monks outlawed for its silences
Golden Yellow, blood of Delilah's throat

No figure but my own: why are you absent
as well as mute? Will you address me at last
in persimmon or lavender? Will you rub my poems
with your thumbs, the way you gauged chartreuse?
Milori Blue, embezzler of horizons   Marlin Blue,
gill slash of the lost ocean

In this field, darknesses grow wings: *Air-gun*
Silver   Licorice Nighthawk   Conquistador Ochre
Primavera Sunset   Viridian Dreamstalk

Father, listen to your son talking in colors!

Charles Adés Fishman

Broich's Boat

It was Frank Broich's boat, thirty-two footer,
three masts and inboard engines, he'd built
with his own hands. It was the boat
and the man — he was the *image*: capable, successful,
sarcastic, brutal — a father — and you, father,
were painfully like him, only less educated, less able
to manipulate the world, but just as violent: quick to whip
off your belt and threaten my life over practically
nothing. You were broad, brawny, bone-weary and bone-
angry from the bequeathed indecencies of your life.

It was Broich's boat that armed me for the next day
at school, for the failure of being your son,
for the shame-faced singularity of growing up.
Those were good hours we spent aboard
that boat: our shared mission, to bring back
a haul of snappers or porgies, white-bellied winter
flounder or "doormat" fluke, to find the mother lode
of fighting blues. Near the buoy, just off the rocks,
on the far side of the toll bridge, the rip tide
would listen to our wills and what we wanted —
adventure, friendship, freedom, even love — might leap
from the green-black swells of ocean and be hooked.

* * *

Father, I want to stand again at starboard as the boat
rocks down, to feel that sluicing energy tear through me
with each ripping nibble, the caution to wait, to pay
out line, the bait taken and run with, the smell of sea brine,
spider crabs, bloodworms drenching — soaking — us,
driving up into our floating bodies.

It is that connection with you I want again, that giving
of your knowledge, your desire — I want to learn from you
again, not a boy at a man's side, anchored by his weight,
his steadiness, but a man in need of you, aware of you.
Before you die, father, fish with me again, share
your secrets: let the tide of our love turn.

Charles Adés Fishman

Saturday Night Two-Step

Mother, you were a child
even in father's arms: you
gave birth to me, a child
still. What loneliness and beauty
you must have known. How
did you make the hours run?
Mother, with your thin eyebrows
and heavy thighs, you have held
me: have come between me
and all women. Once you were
slender, secure in your body:
once you were a world intact,
glowing like a ripe pear at dusk,
musky and lovely. Father loved you:
caressed you and smelled you —
essence of all fruit.

How did you speak to him?
Mother, how did you take
from him what you needed?
this man, so used by life,
so stubborn and ravaged . . .
yet tender with you, *steady*.
Once you were wild about him.
Now you are devoted. How
can I say this to you, mother?

* * *

Father, I will go on talking
while you live, so do not die!
I measure my height by your
shadow. Step into the light!
Such quiet, father. The sun
draws its rays from your heart.
You have always frightened me
a little, as if you might implode
— or explode and shine blindingly.

Once, I was your son and you
rubbed me against the clouds
so I could pull darkness from them.
Your face was warm and rough
and broken — your own face.

Did you love her, father?
I have to know. What did you
desire of her? wish to graft
on her? Father, once you threw me
at the sky, your small wounded
bird. You held me against you
and walked into the sea,
letting the waves rock you,
keeping my face high, lifting me
above you. And she waited
on shore — she who called you
handsome, faithful. You were
a bull in the waves, father.

Charles Adés Fishman

Fathers Are Not Stones

Fathers are not stones, though their voices
may be gravel, their lips granite-white,
nor are they stars set in the black night
to guide us — not stars, not distant suns,
though their light pales with age.

Father, if not stone, why is the path
to your heart so rocky, such a cold climb
to the top? If not star, why do you burn
in sunlight?

Stones are not fathers, nor are sons stars
to warm them when their wrists ache with cold
and their old hips break, when the heat rushes
out of them like a wing in flames.

If not star, a small fire, a saving ledge.
A hand-hold will heal me. If not stone,
then yield your softness. Father, warm me
so I have life to give.

War Story, 1942

I was too young to remember
the year of your heroic fall,
Mama, the strength of purpose
that possessed you when you lost
your footing on the stair but lifted me
above your head, a bundled flag
you would keep from the enemy's hands,
a live bomblet that might explode
upon contact with the planet.
The way you tell it, it took all morning
to fall, as if you had stumbled near the top
of a glacier — had slowly toppled, caught
in a fugue of gravity.
                              Later, you wept.
Your legs had taken the full weight
of your patriot's body: beautiful
Janet Gaynor legs, Lillian Russell legs.
Now you could count your losses:
what motherhood, what marriage had cost
you. Even now, in Florida, as you waltz
with my white-haired father, supported
by his sun-bathed arms, by the charm
of the dance and the music, you feel
the pain of that moment when you knew
I was safe   and you could claim
your wounds.

Charles Adés Fishman

A Toast

I began with poems for you: brass and iron,
poems of zinc, zircon, battered silver, ruby poems,
poems of rust and emerald.

Father, your silence was a mystery I could not
unravel. There seemed to be a somber bridge
you had crossed over, a path of disappearing sunlight
that, forever, had stripped you of words.

Something absent had a crystal grip on you.
Your tenderness was patience, forbearance.
Your nuclear anger scorched all the kite strings
in the kingdom. Yet you taught me how to ride
a golden bike, how to fish for keepers, enduring
in memory as coral, and your pleasure in my life
has slowly healed me, drops of mead licking,
like small cobalt flames, at my heart.

Mother, your girlish laughter always startled,
a song you sang to remember. I was your son
and the air around my body held auroras of sapphire
and opal. You brought me over from the old
country, before life, gave light to me, syllables
for my first human thoughts. Each day was *Un Bel Di*,
tragic and intoxicating, a flash of topaz, then black
onyx fires.

For My Body

In the beginning, the wind lifted you,
your veins rested just beneath the sky.
Do you remember your blood pulsing
fearlessly, a branching tribe of rivers?
Is it true that your hair was curled blond
sunlight? How many falls did you parachute
over? Best friend and most attentive lover,
I remember riding inside you, your winged
leaps and drunken staggers, how you
were stung by beauty, how joy welled up
within you. My body, when your voice
grew dark and smoky as a leaf-strewn glade
and earth-dark hair came to cover you,
your blood surged, you hardened like a wind-
battered pine. Such stretchings and yieldings!
Sunshine and salt spray and the briny fire
of you rising, carrying you with it. Body,
it is still good to know you, to listen
for your sighs, your cries of pain or triumph,
for the rough growls of pleasure in your throat.
But your beard shot through with gray, the first
soft mottlings of black night . . . Old friend,
if you were to find a soul to love your soul, eyes
to adore your eyes, a heart as true as starlight,
gentle as spring's first leaf-green rain — what then?
Would you turn her away, would you turn
from that deep delight?

Charles Adés Fishman

Sun and Rain

*Rain, for food I think you could graze
on horses . . .*

— Mateja Matevski

You are listening to the sun
gather white butterflies.
Gently, that great power descends
and the pale spirits of the grass
rain upward. Daughter, I think you
could dream horses whose wings
spread whitely each morning,
I think you could drink moonbeams.
You know where the night wind wanders,
why the dead remember, who keeps the meadow
green and golden.   In your eyes,
I grow older, but in my heart, a new
and difficult beauty: the child in me saved
at the last turning. Something lifts me again
into the highest branches: I raise my hands
and they are taken. I think for food I could reap
starlight and the heavy silence that wells
between leaves. I think I could love you
in the black mists of Jupiter, the lost seas
of Neptune, the frozen nights of Pluto.

Daughter, you are listening to the rain
chiming our distance, but I am ringing
the bells of the sun.

Mysteries of the Road

Boston. Bright morning. But how
did we get here? Through night
and blizzard, no visibility:
Mysteries of the road.

Now rooftops of neat white sky,
a thick plume of smoke arcing —
each sill and branch fringed
precisely.

Home is a long way off:
eight hours of darkness and ice,
sky of mute answers. Yet
three things clearly proved:

our faith in the next mile,
our trust in each other,
the great power of those who
go out of themselves   to be of use.

Who understands, better than we do,
how it feels to arrive safely —
all the unseen hands guiding,
and our own shaking?

Charles Adés Fishman

Quiet, It's Too Quiet

I.
A neighbor stopped me tonight.
"It's so quiet now," she said.
"Years ago, there were kids
all over the block." Her words
held me. She was right: it's quiet
with you out of the house.
When I work late, there's no one
to worry about — still out,
partying, driving. Silence
follows me upstairs. Your room
is dark   and much too quiet.
It's too quiet at dinner:
your special edge, that rapid-fire
impatience, is missing: a spice
whose absence unmakes the meal.
Too quiet in the den. Even
the bathroom fan is eerily still.

II.
Nothing is quieter than a gull
gliding seaward, except a tern
dreaming on a buoy marker
in the sea's narrow channel.
Nothing is quieter than this
quiet, in which I write to you:

gone from our house. Daughter,
nothing is quieter than this break
in the weather that promises no rain,
low humidity, none of that startling
and clamorous lightning you love —
that lightning you are.

III.
I think of you and I grow quiet,
as I did when you rode in my arms, clung
to my shoulders — I kissed your hair,
the pure beauty of your skull, the bones
of your neck, kissed you and prayed
for you: health, clarity in this life.

IV.
Children play and gulls cry,
but it is much too quiet. Years ago,
you knelt with your toys, held
by their secret voices. I watched you
for hours. Silent as a slow breeze,
I knelt in your pool of silence.

Gold Earrings

Daughter
your gold mornings
rung out by temple bells
wind chimes of darkening temperatures
sudden flare-ups of heat
heat lightning
heat strobing from the deep veins
of your body
heat flashing under your ribs
your childhood melting
like pale ice that has swallowed
sunlight

Blood and Stars

Light from the stars spills
into your eyes, daughter,
blinding you to time, binding
your life to galaxies strewn
beyond our own, changing you
forever. How else explain
your spasms of terror, somber
meditations on desire, your elegies
and exultations — ten-fingered magic
on a theme by Midnight Bach?
That oblivion is in your blood
and in your songs: pain kaleidoscope,
resurrection waltz: that dream Arcadia
five thousand years in the future.
When you sing, the ceiling collapses,
walls peel back: it is fire and storm,
fire and death, the doors to our hearts
shattered. Daughter, it is *fire*,
it is blood and stars.

Charles Adés Fishman

Light in the Afternoon

Fierce hues of summer flowers
in the garden, but what makes a day
take on the colors of memory?

I know, as I write this, daughter,
you wait for my call. It hurts me that you
are injured and I can offer you

only words.

You were the child who wanted
the hard beauty of rubies   their red clamor
and their brooding,

yet I think you are a rose   after all:
that you are strong-willed but fragile
and need a net of loving friends to catch you

when you fall.

The brisk movement of light in the afternoon
sends a chill over grass and brick
and shadows the pool

whose easternmost corner still ripples.
Even the gold throats of daylilies
will soon close   even the sky will fold

its startlingly blue petals.

Father Shaman

Daughter, I am
your witch-doctor tonight
and come to heal you.

I am your medicine man
come to blunt and soften
the jagged blades of lightning
that strike downwards.

I would heal you, child,
would seal your wounds
so not one more drop of your spirit
floods the darkness.

I come this night to repair
all that has been ripped and burned:
I can bear your pain no longer
and bring joy to comfort you   fire
to warm your bones.

Daughter, I am here to anneal
all that has been broken   to calm
and strengthen   to father
your long-delayed renewal.

Speaking Island

I.
Wind seethes deep in the coconut palms,
weaves those spiky leaves into weapons
of samurai rain

then slowly unsheathes the sun — a changeableness
the blood gathers: pelican gulp of the breeze,
blue heron cloaked in mangrove root

and shadow. You drink deeply this moss-tangled
heaven, clasped securely in talons
of sun and air.

II.
From the yellow frangipani, joy in fragrance.
The red hibiscus flares. Welcome to the sun,
to bare skin, the realm of the body,

sweet odors of star-blossoming hands, home
still green and butterfly-golden, aroma
of fresh coffee, vanilla bean, tapioca, ginger.

Your toes and fingers, lips and throat
sing.

III.
What language does the earth speak?
Perhaps tongues near to the equator know
bone-fire Gaelic or Upper Ganges Greek,

some subterranean text darker than Swahili
that bubbles up from a fissure deep
as grief.

It's something about the trees that gives meaning:
the way they sway, the way they lean
toward death.

IV.
And the sea — what vowels or consonants
does the sea utter? Sunlight faltering west
cuts the night to ribbons, prisms of light

risen from the underworld of the moment.
It's the light falling and the slashed night riven
and the mind a full moon tidal in its power:

once again, to be cupped in the palm
of beauty.

Notes

"Beginning with Your Question" is dedicated to Nancy Schoenberger, "A Small Fire" to Mark & Jodie Haselkorn, "Northern Lights" to Mary & Mitch Jacobs, "Far into Vermont" to Leonard & Shirley Rose, "Shanti" to Mary Jacobs, "For Raymond Martin" to Bruce Hartless, "Sand Burial" to Christopher Salonika, "For My Son" to Marlene San Miguel Groner. In the final sequence of poems, "Sun and Rain," "Blood and Stars," "Light in the Afternoon," & "Father Shaman" were written for my daughter, Tamara Fishman, while "Mysteries of the Road," "Quiet, It's Too Quiet" & "Gold Earrings" were written for my daughter, Jillana Esposito. "Speaking Island" is a song and a prayer for both of them.

Cadastral Map: a map showing the boundaries and ownership of land parcels.

C.A.R. ("A Great Silence Has Descended"): Central African Republic.

Hachures: short lines used on maps to shade or to indicate slopes and their degree and direction.

Medicine Wheel Vision (Sect. 3, "Wyoming Nights"): For ninety-six years (1882-1978), the government of this country made the *vision quest* of Native Americans a crime.

"New Orleans Winter": This poem was written in 1981 in the French Quarter of the city, twenty-four years before the advent of Hurricane Katrina.

About the Author

Charles Adés Fishman is Emeritus Distinguished Professor of English & Humanities at Farmingdale State College, where he created the Visiting Writers Program in 1979 and the Distinguished Speakers Program in 2001. He was series editor of the Water Mark Poets of North America Book Award and has served as poetry editor or guest editor for a wide range of publications, among them *Cistercian Studies Quarterly*, *Gaia*, *Journal of Genocide Research*, *New Works Review*, *Pedestal Magazine*, *PRISM: An Interdisciplinary Journal for Holocaust Educators*, and *Shirim*; he has also served as associate editor of *The Drunken Boat* and poetry consultant to the U.S. Holocaust Memorial Museum in Washington, DC. In 1995, Dr. Fishman received a fellowship in poetry from the New York Foundation for the Arts and in 2006, he was honored as "Long Island Poet of the Year" by the Walt Whitman Birthplace Association. His previous books include *Blood to Remember: American Poets on the Holocaust* (2007) and *Chopin's Piano* (2006), both from Time Being Books; *Country of Memory* (Uccelli Press, 2004); and *The Death Mazurka*, a 1989 American Library Association "Outstanding Book of the Year" that was nominated for the 1990 Pulitzer Prize in poetry. *Chopin's Piano* received the 2007 Paterson Award for Literary Excellence.

Made in the USA
Lexington, KY
19 January 2010